^{THE} **Chagres**

POWER OF THE PANAMA CANAL

The Panama Canal was carved through mountains.

THE
CHAGRES
POWER OF THE PANAMA CANAL

by Jean Lee Latham

Illustrations by Louis Glanzman
Maps by Fred Kliem

GARRARD PUBLISHING COMPANY
CHAMPAIGN, ILLINOIS

NANCY LARRICK, ED.D.
IS THE EDUCATIONAL ADVISOR FOR THIS SERIES.

For reading the manuscript of this book and checking the accuracy of its content, the author and editor are grateful to Miles P. DuVal, Jr., Head, Panama Canal Liaison Organization and Isthmian Canal Studies, U.S. Navy Department, 1946-49; Captain of the Port, Balboa, c.a., in charge of marine operations, Pacific Sector, Panama Canal, 1941-44. Author: Panama Canal Series and other writings on inter-oceanic canal history and problems.

Culver Pictures, Inc.

Contents

N
W • E
S

NORTH AMERICA

ATLANTIC OCEAN

SAN FRANCISCO

NEW YORK

PACIFIC OCEAN

5,263 NAUTICAL MILES

CARIBBEAN SEA

PANAMA CANAL

12,000–17,000 NAUTICAL MILES

SOUTH AMERICA

——————— SEA ROUTE FROM
NEW YORK TO SAN FRANCISCO
BEFORE PANAMA CANAL

– – – – – – MODERN SEA ROUTE FROM
NEW YORK TO SAN FRANCISCO
THROUGH THE PANAMA CANAL

U.S. NAUTICAL MILE ... 6,076 FT.
"LAND" OR STATUTE MILE ... 5,280 FT.

CAPE HORN

1. If You Were an Inquiring Reporter

You have heard of the Inquiring Reporter who asks questions of the Man on the Street. Suppose you were an Inquiring Reporter; you asked the Man on the Street, "Where is the Chagres River?" Nine times out of ten he would say, "I don't know." He might make a guess. "Is it in India? Or China?"

The Chagres River is in Panama. It is one of the most important rivers in the world. If there were no Chagres River there would be no Panama Canal. A ship going from New York to San Francisco would have to sail around

Cape Horn on the southern tip of South America. The Chagres River cuts that voyage by almost 8,000 nautical miles—or by almost 9,000 "land" miles.

The Man on the Street generally has mistaken ideas about Panama, too. He pictures it as a narrow strip of land, lying up and down between two oceans, stretching north to south between North and South America. He thinks the Atlantic Ocean is east of Panama and the Pacific Ocean is west of it. He is one hundred per cent wrong. Panama lies between the oceans, stretching west to east between North and South America. The Caribbean Sea, part of the Atlantic, is north of Panama. The Pacific Ocean is south of it. A ship coming from the Atlantic Ocean does not sail west through the Panama Canal. It sails southeast. The Pacific end of the canal is 22 miles east of the Atlantic end.

The Chagres River rises in high mountains in the eastern end of Panama. Its headwaters

are half a mile above sea level. The river bed
is "crooked as a corkscrew." It is fifty miles
as a crow flies from headwaters to mouth, but
the river twists and turns for 120 miles.

For the first half of its course it roars over
waterfalls and foams through rapids, flowing
south toward the Pacific Ocean. By that point
it has dropped from half a mile high to 300
feet above sea level. Now it turns west and
flows more quietly. Then it turns north and
finally empties into the Caribbean Sea. That

A ship sailing from the Atlantic to the Pacific sails SOUTHEAST
through the Panama Canal.

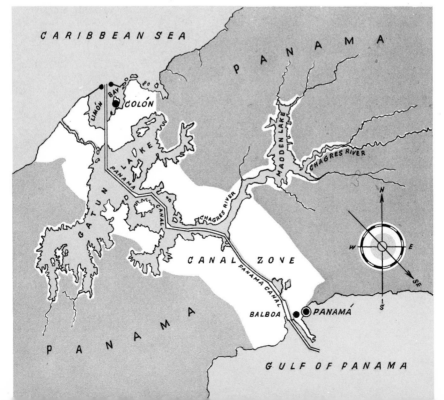

bend to the north in the course of the Chagres has helped write history for more than 400 years.

In the early days the Chagres made a path through green jungle—a waterway that reached within a few miles of the Pacific Ocean.

Today the Chagres supplies the electric power and the water to run the Panama Canal—billions of gallons of water to fill the locks. There are six pairs of those locks—twelve in all. They are huge tanks 1000 feet long and 110 feet wide—more than two and a half times as long as a football field and more than two times as wide as a fifty-foot house lot. More than 12,000 ships pass through the canal each year. There is always enough water to fill the locks. Sometimes there is too much!

For the Chagres rises in one of the rainiest places in the world. As much as thirteen feet of rain falls there each year. Have you ever seen a cloudburst, when rain comes down like a waterfall? Most of the cloudbursts we see do not last very long.   In Chagres country a down-pour like that may last for three days!

When that happens the Chagres may rise 40 feet in 24 hours.   In the great flood of 1923 more than 300,000 gallons of water per second poured from the Chagres into Gatun Lake—more gallons per second than roar down over Niagara Falls.

When the Chagres was behaving itself it was a beautiful river.   When it went on a rampage it was terrifying.   But it was that raging tor-rent of water that made it possible to build the Panama Canal.   The taming of the Chagres makes a fascinating story.   And the Chagres made history for 400 years before the building of the Panama Canal.

2. The Eight-Thousand-Mile Mistake

Columbus was the first white man to see the Chagres River. He found it because of a mistake he made. He discovered America because of that same mistake—a mistake of about 8,000 miles. He thought the world was much smaller than it is. He thought that Europe and Asia, together, stretched almost around the world. He thought Japan was not more than 3,000 miles across the Atlantic from Spain. He did not know the distance was 11,000 miles and that America was in the way. He was not trying to find new lands. He was hunting for a new path to the East. Europe needed a new route.

For hundreds of years before 1492 Europe had traded with the East—with India, Cathay (as they sometimes called China) and the Spice Islands (that they sometimes called the Indies.) Merchants grew rich on trade in silk and cotton, gold and pearls, and spices. They rubbed their hands when they talked of "the riches of Cathay" and "the wealth of the Indies."

The overland journey to the Far East was long and hard—but worth it. One much-traveled route lay through Constantinople. Men said you could stand on a street in Constantinople and see the world pass by. Constantinople was the front door to the East. In 1453 the Turks took Constantinople. They closed the front door to Cathay.

The Portuguese mariners sailed south around

Africa to find a new eastern route to Cathay. Columbus—because of that 8,000-mile mistake, thought the shortest route would be straight west across the Atlantic. He did not promise Ferdinand and Isabella new worlds. He promised a new, shorter route to the Far East. He was hunting for the back door to Cathay.

He sailed west. He came to some islands. He thought they were in the Indies, so he called the brown-skinned natives "Indians." He showed the natives gold and pearls. Did they have those to trade? The Indians pointed south and west. Columbus was sure he was on the right track. On his next voyage he would find that new path to the East!

For ten years Columbus hunted for that path to the East. In 1502 he was on his fourth and last voyage. He reached the coast of what is now Central America.

The Indians pointed south. "There is a narrow place between big waters."

A narrow place between the oceans! At last

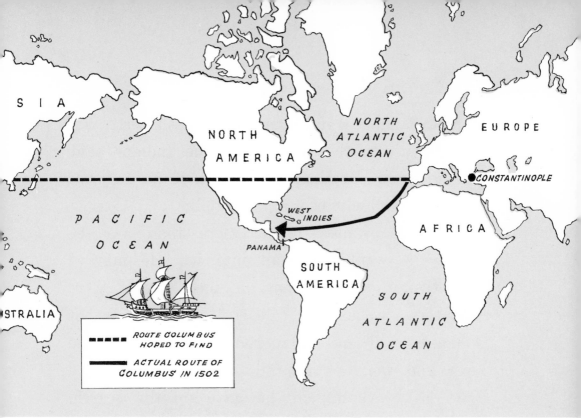

Columbus hoped to reach China by sailing directly west. He did not know a continent blocked his way.

he had found it! Columbus fell on his knees to give thanks. Just to the south was that strait that led to the East! He forgot that there can be two kinds of narrow places between big waters. There can be a strait—a narrow strip of water, making a path; there can be an isthmus—a narrow strip of land barring the way.

He sailed on. He reached the coast of what

15

is now Panama. He came to a wide river. Was it the path to the East? No, the Indians said, but he could *see* the other ocean if he followed the river and climbed a high hill.

Columbus wanted to do more than see the ocean; he wanted to sail into it. He marked the river on his map. Since there were alligators in it he called it the River of Alligators. Then he turned his back on the river and went on hunting for the strait.

At last, heartbroken, he gave up the search. Ten years of struggle—and he had failed. He never knew he had seen the place where the path to the East would be. For the River of Alligators was the Chagres—the river of the Panama Canal.

3. Balboa Makes an Enemy

Seven years passed before white men came again to the Chagres country. In 1509 King Ferdinand sent men to settle there. They had orders to do three things: to build towns, to find gold, and *to find that path to the East!*

At first the Indians welcomed the white men. The natives were glad to trade gold for iron. Gold was just something pretty to use for ornaments and decorations. Iron was useful. They could cut wood with it.

The Spanish got so much gold in trade that they called Chagres country *Castilla del Oro—*

Golden Castile. They were happy with their gold; the Indians were delighted with the iron. Then the Spanish started to build a town. The mood of the Indians changed. Traders—yes! Settlers—no!

The fighting began. The Indians outnumbered the Spanish a hundred to one, but their bows and arrows were no match for the muskets and swords of the white men. The Spanish drove the Indians from their homes and began to build towns on the hot, wet coast. Now to reap the riches of Castilla del Oro!

Then the fevers began. The Spanish sickened and died. But there were always fresh settlers to fill the ranks. Half the newcomers might die in their first month. But the others stayed. There was gold! They would get rich in a year!

So they came—and they died—thousands whose names are forgotten. Three names are remembered from those early days: Balboa, one of the kindest of the Spaniards; Pedrarias and Pizarro, two of the most cruel.

Balboa was the first European to see the Pacific Ocean.

Balboa tried to deal fairly with the Indians. They became his friends. It was an Indian who told Balboa about Peru—a land of gold to the south. It was a young Indian chieftain who led Balboa and his men across Panama to the Pacific Ocean.

One day, as they were crossing the jungle, the young chieftain pointed to a high peak. "Come!"

Balboa climbed. He looked south. In the

distance he saw the shimmering blue of a great ocean. He named it *Mar del Sur* which means "Southern Sea." Five days later he reached the Pacific. Just think what the country must have been like—a five-day journey to reach a place he had seen from a mountain top!

On September 29, 1513, Balboa waded into the Pacific. He took possession of all lands that touched upon it in the name of Spain.

For the moment he gave up the search for the land of gold. He hurried back across Castilla del Oro to send word to Spain about his great discovery.

"When my King knows of this," Balboa thought, "I shall be the most honored man in the world. He will give me ships and men to hunt for the land of gold!"

If there had been a way for Balboa to send his news quickly, his dream might have come true. But before word reached Spain the King had sent a new leader to Castilla del Oro. He was Pedrarias, the cruelest Spaniard who ever set foot in the New World. Men finally called him "Frenisi de Dios"—the Fury of God.

Pedrarias was not pleased with news of Balboa's great discovery. He was savagely jealous. Four years later he had Balboa put to death. He turned a deaf ear on stories of the land of gold to the south.

For almost 20 years he ruled Castilla del Oro. Like many dictators before and after him, he

This old engraving shows Balboa claiming possession of all lands touching the Pacific Ocean.

"got things done"—but at a fearful price. No one knows how many Indians he put to death. Some records say the Indian population sank from 2,500,000 to 500,000 during his rule.

His men explored the southern coast of Castilla del Oro. They found a more healthful region. Pedrarias decided to build his capital there. He heard of a fishing village called Panamá, which means "plenty of fish." Pedrarias drove out the Indians but kept the name. The fishing village grew into a Spanish city with a handsome cathedral, churches, storehouses and many fine homes. Pedrarias ordered a road built from Panamá to the town of Nombre de Dios—Name of God—on a bay on the northern coast.

The Spanish rounded up 4,000 Indians and drove them with whips to build the road. The Indians cleared a path through the jungle and paved it with stones worn smooth from the river-beds. The Spanish called the road Camino Real, the Royal Road. But at first it was little more

than a cobblestone path three feet wide. The
road ran north from Panamá, crossed the
Chagres, and continued north and northeast to
Nombre de Dios.

The Spanish did not have an all-water route
to the Far East, but now they did have a shorter
route. They built a fleet of ships in the Pacific.
These ships sailed to the Far East and brought
their cargoes to Panamá. Then a "shuttle service" of mule trains and slaves carried the
cargoes to Nombre de Dios. There, other ships
carried the cargoes to Spain.

During the rainy season when the Chagres

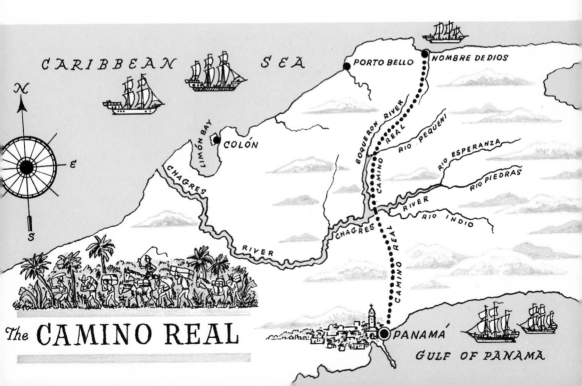

The CAMINO REAL

waters were deeper, the Spanish often loaded cargoes on boats or barges and floated them down the river. Then they sailed east in the Caribbean to Nombre de Dios. It was much farther that way, but a far easier journey. At some time during those years the River of Alligators was called the Chagre. Later—no one knows why—an S was added to the name.

In 1533 Pizarro found that land of gold to the South—Peru. He conquered the Incas. Now more gold than the world had ever seen followed the shuttle service across Castilla del Oro.

The Spanish cleared sunken logs and sandbars from the Chagres. They built ventas, or inns, on its banks. More and more cargoes followed the winding route of the river.

From time to time the Spaniards thought of that short distance overland from the Chagres to the Pacific. From time to time they talked of digging a canal to the Great South Sea. King Philip II of Spain was the man who said "No!" to the idea of a canal.

4. The Buccaneers

Philip II came to the throne of Spain in 1558. He ruled his New World colonies with an iron hand. They could trade with no ships but his; they must send their goods to the ports he chose.

Foreign ships began to prowl the Caribbean and the Gulf of Mexico to trade with the Spanish colonists. The foreign smugglers made things much easier for the colonists. Soon a thriving trade sprang up.

The foreign ships began to do more than trade with the colonists. They attacked the ships of the treasure fleet of Spain. Moreover, they represented another possible danger. What if they captured Nombre de Dios and Panamá and took over the treasure route? So when there was talk of a canal across Castilla del Oro, Philip said "No!" A canal might make it too easy for a foreign nation to take over the treasure route.

For over a hundred years Spain fought to guard her treasure route. She moved her northern port from Nombre de Dios to Porto Bello—a place that was easier to fortify. She built forts at Porto Bello. She built another to guard the mouth of the Chagres. She armed the forts with her biggest guns and manned them with her best soldiers. Still the foreign raiders made trouble.

One habit of the raiders must have had the Spanish gnashing their teeth. The favorite diet on raiding ships was Spanish beef.

In the early days the Spanish had brought

Still standing at Porto Bello are ruins of an old Spanish fort, San Geronimo.

cattle to this area. Now there were great herds of cattle running wild. Every so often a shipload of raiders put in at some deserted cove along the coast. The raiders went ashore, killed wild cattle, cut the beef into strips and "boucanned" it—smoked it over fires of green wood.

Soon the raiders were called "buccaneers" because of the "boucanned" meat they ate. (Just as the British sailors of a later day would be called "limeys" because of the limes they used to prevent scurvy.)

27

In 1671 a buccaneer named Henry Morgan finally succeeded in crossing Castilla del Oro. He captured the city of Panamá. For days his men looted the city of gold and jewels. Only one treasure escaped them—a huge Altar of Gold in the cathedral. The Spanish had covered it with a coat of black paint, so that it looked like wood. The buccaneers did not bother with it. Who cared about a clumsy piece of carved wood?

At last the buccaneers set out for the northern coast. Behind them fires smoldered. Soon nothing was left of Panamá but a few blackened walls of stone rising from the ashes. Walls— and the Altar of Gold.

The Spanish moved to another place and built Panamá again. This time, they would build walls so strong and high that Panamá would never fall!

The cost of those walls shocked the King. For days he could only shake his head and mutter. One day someone saw him standing at a

28

The Altar of Gold is a treasure English pirates missed.

window in his castle in Spain, staring west through a telescope.

"What is His Majesty looking for?" the man asked.

"For the walls of New Panamá," the King said. "They cost so much I should be able to see them from here!"

The English became more and more powerful in the Caribbean. They harried the Spanish fleets. At last Spain gave up the Chagres route

In Porto Bello are these ruins of a customs house where the Spaniards once stored gold.

and sent her ships south around Cape Horn.

But England did not gain a foothold on the coast. Time and again she almost succeeded, then went down to defeat. Spain did not stop her. The Chagres country did. Where one man died in battle, a hundred died of the fevers.

No one knew what caused the fevers. Man blamed one kind on *mal aire*—bad air. So they called it malaria. They called a second kind Chagres fever. They called a third kind yellow fever. They dreaded it most of all.

The English had driven Spain from the Chagres route; the fevers drove the English out. Then Castilla del Oro went back to sleep. No mule bells tinkled on the overland trail. No treasure-laden barges came down the Chagres. The jungle took back its world. It swallowed the trail, the way stations and the ventas. As far as eye could see there was only unbroken green. Only the Chagres made a path through the jungle—a path that reached within a few miles of the Pacific.

5. Gold!

In 1802—three hundred years after Columbus saw the Chagres—another great explorer was there—the Baron von Humboldt. The book of his explorations became a best seller. Among other things he talked of the need of a canal to join the Atlantic and the Pacific.

Finally Spain woke up. Maybe Philip II had been wrong. Maybe there should be a canal. She began to plan. But it was too late for Spain. Her colonies in the New World were rebelling. In a few years she lost almost every possession in the Americas. One place she still held was the island of Cuba.

By 1848 the United States owned all the one-time Spanish lands west of the Mississippi and north of the Rio Grande. The country spread from New York to California.

"Much good it will do us!" some men said. "California is farther away than England! Three thousand miles to England; thirteen thousand miles around Cape Horn from New York to California!"

Some daring New York merchants decided to shorten that voyage to California. They founded two steamship lines. The Atlantic line ran from New York to the Chagres. The Pacific line ran from Panamá to San Francisco. Once more there was a shuttle service across Panama. A man took passage to the Chagres, then hired a cayuca, a dugout canoe, to take him as far up the river as possible. He finished the journey on mule-back to Panamá, then boarded a steamer for California.

But men had heard of the Chagres fevers. Many said nobody could pay them enough to go that way. For a time it looked as though the steamship companies would fail. Then gold was discovered in California. Gold!

Now the cry was "California or bust!" Men stopped talking of Chagres fever. Business boomed on the steamship lines.

Men asked for "your best private cabin" on a steamer, got a bunk in a cabin with nine other passengers, raised cain about it, but went anyhow. It was the quickest way to California.

Sometimes when a ship came to anchor off the Chagres the passengers had to wait for hours or even days before the water was calm enough for them to land. Natives in dugouts had to take them from the ship to a little settlement of pineboard shacks on the west bank of the Chagres.

There the forty-niners jostled and shouted, trying to outbid each other for the first dugout up the Chagres. The natives smiled to themselves and let the *Yanquis* bid. No one but a native could handle those dugouts. Already they were

getting twice as much money for the trip up-river as they had at first.

The last dugout to start upriver had eight passengers and their luggage. Two natives clad in ragged trousers stood in the dugout, pushing lazily with long poles.

A lanky young farm lad from New England sat in the dugout and thought of stony New England farms. He stared at the sparkling water, then at the lush green on the riverbanks.

He thought of the girl who was waiting back home for him. "Wish Samantha could see it," he thought. "A body can hardly believe it!"

Those huge trees, rising straight from the water's edge—those huge vines, big around as a man's arm—they must have been there for a thousand years! Year in, year out, nothing to do but grow. No drought to burn it. No freeze to stop it. Just green forever. And the flowers! So big a man couldn't believe them, either! "Flowers as big as dinner plates and butterflies as big as saucers!" That's what he'd tell her! He thought of the mosquitoes the night before. "And mosquitoes as big as sparrows!"

Afternoon came. The boatmen began to watch the sky. Suddenly they nodded to each other. The dugout shot over the water to the river-bank, under the trees. A gust of chilly wind, then the lightning, the thunder and the rain. The Chagres rose and foamed past them. The boatmen grabbed the overhanging branches and held the boat against the riverbank. The rain stopped. The Chagres calmed down as quickly as it had risen.

That evening the young man stood on the bank of the river and watched the sunset—a brief blaze of glory soon swallowed by darkness. "Smothers it like a horse blanket!" he'd tell Samantha. Some day they'd make this trip together!

Two days later he sat astride a mule so small that the man's legs almost dragged on the ground. The mule clambered up a steep slope like a cat. Then he pulled his hoofs together and slid down the other side of the ridge. It

wasn't until afternoon that he hit a mudhole, belly deep, and slipped. He went one way, the young man the other. The mule scrambled out of the mud and stood patiently waiting.

The man perched on his saddle, his feet propped on either side of the mule's neck, his knees sticking out. "Like a grasshopper's elbows!" he thought.

In Panamá he had to wait for the steamer. The captains on the Pacific run were having trouble. Their crews would jump ship in San Francisco and join the forty-niners.

The young man spent his time writing to Samantha. It was slow work. Besides, he didn't feel good. The last thing he wrote was about the trail. "It's impossible! Something's got to be done about it! I'm going to talk to people."

He was dead the next morning. Sometimes yellow fever struck quickly. They burned his letter. Nobody knew how yellow fever was spread. They couldn't risk sending it.

Others besides the young farm lad were

thinking that something had to be done about the Chagres route. Mr. William Henry Aspinwall, head of the Pacific Steamship Company, was organizing a company to build a railroad across Panama.

First, they must get permission. That must come from New Granada, the country just east of Panama. The relation between Panama and New Granada was an off-again-on-again affair. But just now Panama belonged to New Granada.

"I'll need a man who knows those people," Mr. Aspinwall told himself. He thought of John Lloyd Stephens, world traveler, writer and lecturer who had spent years in Central and South America.

Mr. Aspinwall picked the right man. Mr. Stephens went to Bogotá, the capital of New Granada. He got the permission. The Panama Railroad Company could build their tracks from Panamá to whatever spot they chose on the Caribbean.

"Porto Bello is the best place," Mr. Stephens

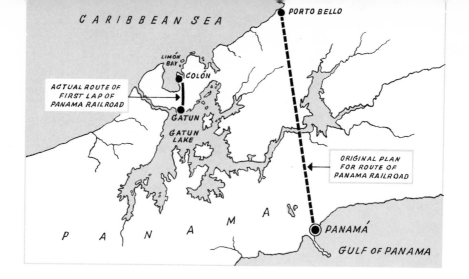

said. "We'll run our tracks from there to the Chagres, then follow the valley as far as possible. I don't believe the route will be more than 50 miles long. We ought to be able to build it for a million dollars."

The company had no trouble raising the money. Businessmen said they were "very clever fellows" to plan a railroad across Panama.

The company hired engineers to build the road. Mr. Stephens went to Panama with them. "We'll start at Porto Bello," he said.

But another "very clever fellow" from New York had got there ahead of them. He had bought up all the land around Porto Bello. Did they want a right-of-way across his land? They could have it—at a price. The price he asked was impossible. What could they do?

"The next best harbor," Mr. Stephens said, "is in Limón Bay. We'll start our tracks on Manzanillo Island, out in the bay. Then we'll fill in earth from Manzanillo to the mainland and run our tracks over the filled land."

In May, 1850, Mr. Stephens and the engineers hired boats to take their camping equipment and instruments to the island. They stepped ashore— and sank in mud up to their knees. The island was an atoll, a coral ring. Only the shoreline was firm. The rest of the island was slimy ooze, crawling with alligators, snakes and scorpions and swarming with mosquitoes.

One thing sure, they could not camp on the island! Mr. Stephens found a deserted steamer, had her cleaned and repaired and hauled around to the island. "We'll live on her for a few weeks," he said, "till we fill in Manzanillo."

It took more than "a few weeks." Ton after

ton of rock disappeared into the slimy ooze. It was August before they could build a work camp on Manzanillo. How long before they could build railroad tracks? And . . . how long would their money last?

In November of 1851 the engineers sat in a shack on Manzanillo and wordlessly looked at each other. Eighteen months of heartbreaking work, and they had built just eight miles of track, to Gatun on the bank of the Chagres. Eight miles of track—and they had spent the whole million dollars!

"We're ruined," one said. "Only a miracle can save us now."

The wind began to howl like a banshee. A hurricane! Before morning they'd probably be washed into the sea and drowned.

Morning came. The storm had passed. They were still alive. Not that it was going to do them much good. They ate, then went out to board a flatcar to ride over to Gatun.

They heard shouts. Two steamers full of

forty-niners were anchored off Manzanillo. Last night in the hurricane the ships had fled from the mouth of the Chagres to Limón Bay.

A forty-niner pointed to the tracks. "How far do you go?"

"Just eight miles," an engineer said. "To Gatun on the Chagres."

"Take us!" the forty-niners shouted. No passenger cars? What of it? They'd ride the flat-cars!

"But we don't know what to charge you!"

"Name a price! We'll pay it!"

The engineers named an outlandish price—enough to get rid of the bothersome forty-niners. "Fifty cents a mile. And ten cents a pound for baggage."

With a whoop and a holler the forty-niners agreed. It took all morning to shuttle two ship-loads to Gatun. When the last flatcar disappeared with its load the engineers began to count the money. The miracle had happened! The railroad was saved!

After that all steamers came to Manzanillo. The forty-niners rode as far as the tracks were laid, then finished the journey by boat up the Chagres and by mule trail to Panamá.

The money problem was solved, but not the problem of workmen. Newcomers arrived, sickened and died. Some brought other diseases with them—cholera and bubonic plague.

Men called Chagres country "the pesthole of the world." But still the forty-niners came, and business boomed on the railroad that was still a-building.

For two years Mr. Stephens stayed there with the engineers. Then he went north for a little vacation. He'd be back soon, he promised.

In November a steamship captain brought the news. Mr. Stephens had died—probably of cholera. The railroad had taken one more life.

In 1855 the last rails were laid and the last spikes driven. The Panama Railroad was built— but at what a price! It had cost $8,000,000 and no one knew how many lives.

But men could cross Panama more quickly now—in four hours instead of in four to eight days. The most costly railroad in the world became the richest.

Fourteen years later, in 1869, two things happened that were going to affect the world's richest railroad. Far north in the United States the last spike was driven in the first transcontinental railroad. Now the shortest and best route from New York to California was not by Panama; it was across the United States.

The other thing happened in Egypt. Ferdinand

De Lesseps, promoter of the Suez Canal, saw the first ship sail from the Mediterranean to the Red Sea. He had cut the voyage from England to India by 6,000 miles.

Soon De Lesseps was getting interested in Panama. He saw surveys that had been done of the region. It was very different country from the land around the Suez Canal, but De Lesseps did not think much about that. He had built a sea-level canal at Suez; he would build a sea-level canal at Panama. Mountains? What of them? His engineers would cut down through them!

Engineers tried to argue with De Lesseps. One of the most brilliant of the French engineers, Adolph Godin De Lépinay, wrote a long report about the problem of a sea-level canal in Chagres country. What were they going to do with the Chagres River? Had they ever seen it on a rampage? Why not use the river? Why not dam it, make a big lake, and use locks to lift the ships from sea level to the lake and down again? Many years later, the United States built the Panama Canal very much as De Lépinay had planned it.

But De Lesseps paid no attention to the report. By 1880 the French engineers were in Panama, surveying the route for a sea-level canal. They knew it was going to be a terrific undertaking. It was going to cost a lot of money. They added up the cost and gave the figures to De Lesseps. He did not take their word for that, either. He slashed several hundred thousand dollars off the figures.

The French canal was doomed before work began. Not enough money was raised. Much of the money they did raise was wasted in crooked deals.

Mosquitoes were another problem—the mosquitoes that carried malaria and yellow fever. When white strangers came to Panama, one out of every three died.

The Chagres made trouble, too. Every so often it went on a rampage, sweeping away houses, washing out bridges and railroad tracks.

At last the French decided they must change their plans. But it was too late. The canal company was too heavily in debt. In 1889 the company went bankrupt. The French government began to investigate. The scandals that were uncovered rocked the nation and sent quite a few men to prison. De Lesseps lost his mind and died.

The French stopped work at Panama. Once more the jungle took over, swallowing acres of machinery and hundreds of houses. Panama went back to sleep. The only thing that moved swiftly was the Chagres, when it went on one of its rainy-season rampages.

Cartoon of De Lesseps shows the public criticism of the French canal project.

IS M. DE LESSEPS A CANAL DIGGER OR A GRAVE DIGGER?

The jungle had taken over.

6. Rebellion in Panama

The first French Canal Company had failed. But the French did not give up hope. They kept a small force of men at Panama, planning how they could build the canal—someday. They studied the rampages of the Chagres so they would know how to tame the river—someday— when they had money enough to build the canal. Finally the French realized that their "someday" was never coming. They could not raise the money to build the canal. They saw only one chance to get back any of the millions they had spent at Panama. That one chance was to sell their rights in Panama to the United States.

People of the United States had often talked of a canal. Some were for it, some against it. In the late 1890's they were paying more attention to the situation in Cuba. For years the Cuban people had been trying to throw off the harsh rule of Spain. The newspapers in the United States sympathized with the Cubans. Finally even the Man on the Street was saying that something ought to be done. Just what, he did not know—but something.

In 1898 news about two battleships roused the whole United States. The *U.S.S. Maine* went to Cuba to protect United States citizens during an uprising. She was blown up in Havana Harbor. How it happened no one knows, but the people of the United States blamed Spain. Now the cry was "Remember the *Maine!*" and the Spanish-American War began.

What happened to the *U.S.S. Oregon* stirred people, too. She was "The Ship That Wasn't

There." Our navy got word that a Spanish fleet was steaming toward Cuba. We needed to rush our ships there to meet the threat. And where was one of our biggest ships? The *Oregon* was in the Pacific, off California. Luckily telegraph lines spanned the country. We could order her to come. But—the *Oregon* had to come by that long route around Cape Horn.

That was when the United States woke up. "Remember the *Maine!*" started the war; "Remember the *Oregon!*" started everybody thinking about the need for a canal. And after the war a group of army doctors and a Cuban doctor solved the problem of yellow fever.

The Cuban doctor had the odd name of Carlos Juan Finlay. His father was a Scotsman. For twenty years Dr. Finlay had said that one mosquito, the female stegomyia, spread yellow fever.

"She is a delicate and fussy lady, this mosquito," Dr. Finlay said. "She likes clean, still water in or near homes. She cannot fly far. So get rid of clean, standing water around homes, fumigate the houses, and shut yellow fever patients away from her with screens. You will wipe out yellow fever!"

For 20 years other doctors had laughed off Dr. Finlay's ideas. At first, the Yellow Fever Board under Dr. Walter Reed did not believe him, either. But finally they listened. The whole story of their work—the men who risked their lives to test Dr. Finlay's ideas—the man who died— is too long to tell here. When you read it you will never forget it.

The United States Army ordered one of their doctors, William C. Gorgas, to carry out Dr. Finlay's ideas in Havana. Dr. Gorgas did—and wiped out yellow fever!

Stegomyia mosquito

Major General William C. Gorgas, who conquered yellow fever in Havana.

Meantime, another doctor, Ronald Ross of the British army, had solved the mystery of malaria. It was not due to "mal aire"—bad air. It was spread by another mosquito, the anopheles.

By 1901 the United States was talking seriously of a canal. But they were planning to dig it in Nicaragua instead of in Panama.

Naturally the French were upset. Was all their work to go for nothing? The French fought desperately to persuade the United States to build at Panama. At last Congress voted: The United

States would build a canal at Panama—*or* at Nicaragua—*if*. The *if* was in two parts: *If* the French would sell their rights and all their property in Panama for $40,000,000; *if* Colombia would sign a treaty, turning over a strip of land in Panama to the United States. The French agreed; Colombia refused to sign the treaty.

Then the people of Panama were upset. They had looked forward to being the Crossroads of the World. Was progress going to make a detour around them? For a long time Panama had resented the rule of Colombia. In the last fifty-odd years there had been more than fifty uprisings. Now Panama was ready to rebel and break the ties with Colombia forever.

November 3, 1903, Panama won its independence. November 18, 1903, Panama and the United States signed a treaty. It granted the United States sovereignty over a zone of land ten miles wide across Panama—absolute control of it "in perpetuity"—forever. The two cities, Colón on

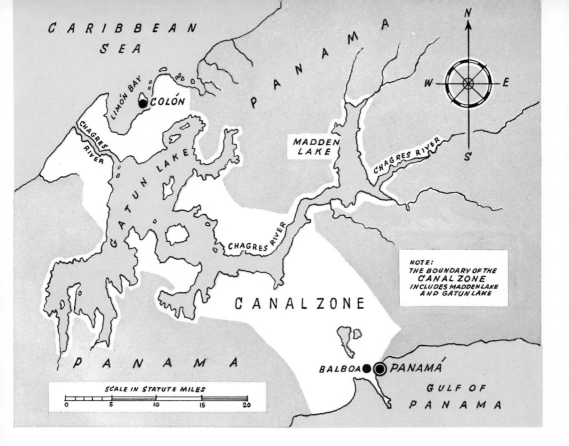

Manzanillo Island, and Panamá, would belong to Panama, but the United States would have the right to take care of health problems in both cities.

President Theodore Roosevelt knew that health problems must come first. And he had the doctor who could stamp out yellow fever—Dr. William C. Gorgas.

7. Problems in Panama

Early in 1904 Dr. Gorgas went to Panama. He saw the conditions in Panamá and Colón—no paved streets, no running water, no sewers—filth and garbage everywhere.

But he was not looking at the dirt. He was looking at the catch basins on the roofs of all the houses. People caught water in them to use during the dry season. That, he knew, was one place the stegomyia was breeding. Before he could get rid of yellow fever, he had to get rid of standing water. Before he could do that, he would have to pipe running water to both cities.

57

Cathedral belfry
overlooks the older
part of Panamá.

Courtesy of United Fruit Company

He made out a list of the supplies he needed— miles of pipe for running water and sewers— thousands of feet of copper screen. He had to send his order to the seven-man commission in Washington. The commission promised to "consider" his requests. Weeks passed. No supplies came.

Mr. Wallace, chief engineer, wrote for the "plant" he needed—the machines to do the job. The commission "considered" his requests, too. Months passed.

Meantime, all the papers in the north were hammering on one thing: *Let's see the dirt fly!* What was going on down at Panama? Why weren't they digging that canal?

Mr. Wallace groaned. He was not ready to begin to dig. But he felt he had to "make the dirt fly." He repaired some of the out-of-date French machines and started digging at Culebra Cut. That was where a man-made gorge, nine miles long, had to be dug through the highest mountains the canal would cross.

P.I.P. Photo by Ullstein

A cemetery in Colón holds the graves of thousands of Canal workers.

New workmen began coming in—strangers to Panama. Dr. Gorgas looked at them and prayed. He should have wiped out yellow fever by now. He knew he had not.

Yellow fever began to spread. And panic spread even faster. Every time one man died, fifty men fled to Colón and tried to get passage on a ship going north. Work slowed to a crawl.

News from Washington was bad; the first commission had resigned. What would happen now? Chief Engineer Wallace went to Washington. Could he straighten things out? The next news was even worse; Mr. Wallace had resigned, too.

"We're through!" the men at Panama said. "The next thing we'll hear is to leave Panama. We've failed!"

Instead, two new men came to Panama. One was Mr. Shonts, chairman of the new commission. The other was John F. Stevens, the new chief engineer. They were both railroad men—used to doing big things—used to giving orders and having them carried out without questions.

"We've promised to try to straighten out this mess," Mr. Shonts said. "We both came down here on one condition: we'll not answer to anybody, high or low, but to the President. Mr. Stevens has built railroads through wild country. We think he'll know what to do. I'll be going back to Washington soon, to keep things moving at that end. I'll depend on you men down here to ask for what you need. You'll get it."

. Mr. Stevens was a big, calm man with the look of a born leader and a sense of humor. He covered the Canal Zone from Colón to Panamá.

He looked at the docks, loaded with cargo; he looked at the work camps—such as they were, and the railroad—such as it was. It took him just one week to size up the situation.

"We'll stop this idiotic digging until we are ready to dig," he said.

"With the papers back home screaming for us to 'make the dirt fly'?" Dr. Gorgas asked.

"We'll let them scream," Mr. Stevens drawled. "There are three diseases down here—malaria, yellow fever and cold feet. The worst is cold feet. We'll stamp out yellow fever first. Then we'll get ready to take care of our workmen."

In the next few months, between them Dr. Gorgas and Mr. Stevens spent $30,000,000. Yellow fever was wiped out. Panamá and Colón had paved streets, running water and screens.

Mr. Stevens was ready for his workmen. There were decent quarters for them to live in, a commissary department to feed them and clubhouses where men far from home could gather when the day's work was done.

Panamá today is a modern city of over 200,000 inhabitants.

He had the "plant" for them to work with,
too—the biggest and most powerful equipment to
do the job. He had rebuilt most of the Panama
Railroad—"a phantom railroad" was what he
called it—with heavier rails, double-tracked much
of the way, to handle traffic without delay.

An efficient railroad system was the key to

building the canal. Thousands of men had to depend on the railroad to take them to and from their jobs, and for their food and the supplies for their work. The digging at Culebra Cut depended on the railroad, too. Steam shovels could lift tons of "spoil"—the earth and rock—in one bite. But trains had to be there, on schedule, to haul the spoil away.

Mr. Stevens had brought order out of chaos; "cold feet" no longer threatened the canal with failure. But now another danger hung over it—a more serious one.

A board of engineers were debating the most important question: Should we build a sea-level canal, or a high-level canal with locks leading up to a lake? More than 20 years before, the French engineer De Lépinay had said that the only hope of success was a high-level canal. After a short time in Panama, Mr. Stevens agreed with De Lépinay. But the board of engineers voted, eight to five, in favor of a sea-level canal.

Mr. Stevens knew he had a fight on his hands.

And for the next six months he fought "the battle of the levels"—first with the President, and finally with Congress. The end of June, 1906, Congress voted in favor of the high-level canal.

Mr. Stevens probably sighed with relief when he could go back to Panama. Twice he had interrupted his work to come to Washington over the "battle of the levels." Now he could get back on the job!

By early 1907 he had made unbelievable strides. Details were so well worked out that he could say, "The canal will be open by January of 1915." He had the plant they needed; he had the workmen. Probably most amazing of all, he had planned how to handle all the trains—from 450 to 550 a day—so that everything could move without interruption.

He was *the* man of Panama. Then John F. Stevens resigned.

8. Men Against the Mountains

Both Mr. Shonts, chairman of the canal commission, and Mr. Stevens resigned. President
Roosevelt could not argue with them about it.
Both men had told the President the same sort
of thing: "I'll not promise to stay to the end of
the job; I'll stay until I can see the end."

No—the President could not argue, but he
could make a vow: "I'm done with men who can
resign. I'll send men who *have* to stay!" And
he ordered an army engineer, Colonel George W.
Goethals, to take charge, both as chief engineer
and as chairman of the canal commission. That,

so far as the President was concerned, was that!

But it did not settle things in Panama. The workmen were up in arms. They'd do anything for Mr. Stevens. But take orders from the army? Never!

Colonel Goethals had known he was taking on a big job of engineering. When he got to Panama, he soon realized the problem of the workmen was going to give him more trouble.

He packed his uniforms in mothballs. He changed to white duck suits and a straw hat. He went to a meeting to talk to the men. "I am no longer a commander in the United States Army," he said. "I am commanding the Army of Panama. The enemy we are going to defeat is the Culebra Cut and the locks and dams to control the Chagres River. No man here, who is doing his job well, has anything to fear from the military. Any man who has anything to complain about may come and tell me. I'll be in my office every Sunday morning. First come, first served."

The first Sunday morning a Jamaican Negro

came with his wife. He had a complaint. His wife had earned money doing washing. She would not give it to him—her husband. As a British subject, he had a right to that money!

"We can take care of that very easily," the colonel said. "I can send you back to Jamaica. There you can enjoy your rights as a British subject."

The man scratched his head. Maybe he was thinking about his wages at Panama—five times what he could earn at home. "I'd rather stay!"

The colonel beamed. "We'll be glad to have you!"

Word of the Sunday court must have spread rapidly. The next time the colonel visited the men on the job some of them actually smiled at him.

Now he could give more attention to the engineering problems of his job—the biggest engineering feat that man had ever undertaken.

No man appreciated Mr. Stevens' work more than Colonel Goethals. Once the colonel said:

"The real problem of digging the canal was disposal of the spoil, and no army engineer in America could have laid out the transportation scheme as Mr. Stevens did. We are building on the foundation he laid, and the world cannot give him too much credit."

The biggest job of moving spoil would be at Culebra Cut. The engineers thought, in 1907, they knew how big the job was. But the mountains at Culebra had a few surprises in store for them.

Mr. Stevens had prepared the way for the work at Culebra. Thanks to him the Americans could move spoil five times as fast as the French. They did this not because they were better engineers or because they had better workmen. They did it with machinery that had not been invented in the days of the French canal work.

For instance, there was the matter of blasting to loosen the spoil. The French could sink only a small hole, or shaft, put in a few pounds of dynamite, light a fuse, then get out of the way

Culebra Cut during the French canal work.

in a hurry. The Americans had rock drills that could sink a hole 27 feet deep; 300 of those rock drills dug 90 miles of holes every month. The Americans could set off ten to twenty tons of dynamite in one blast.

The French had to use twice as much dynamite to break up the spoil as the Americans did. A stone weighing 150 to 200 pounds was as big as a workman could handle. The Americans had huge steam shovels that could lift a boulder weighing ten to twelve tons. The steam shovels

69

American steam shovel loading rock in 1911.

chewed into the spoil, taking a five- to seven-ton bite every two or three minutes and loading it onto a flatcar.

As Colonel Goethals said, the real problem of digging the canal was getting rid of the spoil. Before they were done with the job they made miles of solid land in marshes. That was before the days of dump trucks that can plow over any kind of ground, tilt their beds and dump a load. At Panama they had to use railroads to handle the spoil and that meant cars running on tracks. So they had three things to do where they dumped the spoil: First they unloaded the flat-cars, leaving a long ridge of earth beside the tracks; then they leveled the earth and tamped it until they had solid land; then they had to take up the tracks and move them sideways and put them together again on the new land so they could begin to dump on the next strip of marshland.

The French had to use a swarm of workmen to unload the cars by hand. The Americans had

Flatcars unloaded the spoil in the marshes where it was tamped. Then the tracks were moved over and the operation repeated.

huge flatcars with one high side and one open side. The ends of the cars could be laid flat, making an apron that extended from one car to the next. When a train was ready to be unloaded it looked like an iron shelf 30 cars long. No workmen had to unload the spoil. Machinery dragged a three-and-a-half-ton plow the length of the shelf, unloading the cars in one sweep.

The French workmen had to level the ridge of earth by hand. The Americans had a big spreader that worked as fast as the unloader, and did the work of 250 men.

The job that took the most time was moving the tracks. It took 600 workmen to move one mile of track a day, pulling up spikes, lifting rails, moving the crossties and putting the track together again. The Americans used a track shifter invented by Mr. William G. Bierd, a railroad man. Nine men, operating the track shifter, could lift the track, all in one piece, and move it sideways as much as nine feet. They could do as much work as 600 men.

The track shifter greatly helped to speed the work of the Americans.

Panama Canal Information Office

The Americans had 300 rock drills, 105 steam shovels, 30 unloaders, 26 spreaders, 9 track shifters, 161 huge locomotives, 1700 flatcars and 1800 dump cars. No wonder they could move spoil so fast. People said "they can move mountains!"

Then they found that the mountains could move dirt, too—in slides. Some of the slides broke off suddenly and thundered down like an avalanche, pouring hundreds of tons of spoil into the cut, burying steam shovels, trains, tracks—everything. In a few minutes they could wipe out a month's work.

73

The avalanches were the smaller slides. The big ones moved like glaciers. Far back of Culebra Cut a long crack would open in the earth, parallel to the cut. Then acres of land began to move and kept on moving day after day and week after week. One slide covered 47 acres; the biggest one—men called it Cucaracha—the cockroach—covered 75 acres. Before Culebra Cut was done 225 acres of slides had poured into it. Month after month, year after year, the men at Culebra fought the battle of the slides.

Colonel Gaillard, engineer in charge at Culebra, finally seemed to be getting edgy. Was he losing his nerve? He began to look downright sick. At last he went home "for a little rest." Later the sad news reached Culebra. Colonel Gaillard had died of a brain tumor. No wonder he had seemed "a little edgy"! They knew now he had never "lost his nerve." He had fought a great fight as long as he possibly could. That is why Culebra Cut is named Gaillard Cut in his memory.

9. Men Against the River

In 1906 Congress had voted for the high-level canal with three sets of locks, one at Gatun in the Atlantic end of the canal and two sets in the Pacific end separated by the small Miraflores Lake. The heart of that canal would be the larger Gatun Lake, made by damming the Chagres River. The work of damming the Chagres began that summer under Mr. Stevens and went on for years . . . and years.

First there was the question of where to build the dam. Gatun, the narrowest part of the valley, looked like a good choice—if engineers found the right sort of earth to bear the weight of the dam. No man knew what the earth might be like. What kind of valley had the Chagres carved through the ages?

Men had to clear almost 600 acres of jungle before they knew. Then how they must have cheered! What had that wild, magnificent river done to help them? It had carved a valley a mile-and-a-half wide and had left a hill of solid rock in the middle of the valley at a perfect place to build the spillway for the dam!

But there were other things the engineers had to know before they could plan the dam and make the lake. Surveyors had one of the hardest jobs to do. They had to measure the height and shape of every mountain ridge and gorge for almost 200 square miles. The engineers had to know exactly where the Chagres was going to go when they dammed it.

There were no roads into the country that had to be surveyed. Natives took the surveyors as far as they could up the Chagres and its tributaries. Then the natives swung their machetes, hacking the way through the jungle. No one could go inland from the rivers without hacking a trail.

Every so often a native would bring a dugout back downriver with a surveyor lying in the bottom of it. They were working in country swarming with mosquitoes. Even forty grains of quinine a day could not ward off an attack of malaria forever. Sooner or later a surveyor was flat on his back. Then a native brought him downriver, carried him to the hospital and took another surveyor up to join the crew on the job.

At last the malaria-ridden surveyors finished their work and brought in their maps. The engineers had the information they needed. They could find out the size and shape of the lake they would make. It would be very irregular in shape—looking something like a pressed chrysanthemum—as the river poked fingers of water into dozens of gorges between mountains. The lake would cover 164 square miles and hold 183 billion gallons of water when it was filled to 85 feet

Gatun Spillway under construction, showing openings for steel gates.

above sea level. Ships could sail across the lake from the Gatun locks on the north to Culebra Cut and on to the locks on the south.

Next, the engineers studied all the records of the floods of the Chagres. How many gates in the spillway, and how big must they be, to let out the excess water when the Chagres went on a rampage? The engineers had a lot of respect for the Chagres! The spillway has fourteen steel gates, each weighing 22 tons, and 20 feet wide and 45 feet high. The gates move up and down like windows. One, two, or all can be opened when a lake covering 164 square miles does not make enough room for the Chagres.

(A few years later, at Alhajuela, above Gatun Lake, engineers dammed the Chagres again and made Madden Lake. It is much smaller than Gatun—only 19 square miles—but much deeper. It can furnish over 19 billion cubic feet of water each year—almost one-fourth of the water needed to run the canal. Moreover, its power plant can furnish 8,000 kilowatts of electricity. And—what is also important—Madden Lake can control 5.5 billion cubic feet of extra water during a flood. The engineers soon learned to respect the power of the Chagres on a rampage!)

Before the engineers could start building Gatun Dam they had to provide a temporary detour for the Chagres. They dug a big channel and turned the Chagres into that.

At last the day came when they were ready to turn the Chagres back into its original channel. To do this they had to put a dam across the

Madden Dam furnishes additional water for lockages, control of floods and power for running the Canal.

opening of the detour. This was the first attempt to dam the Chagres.

They did not expect any trouble. They could dump mountains of rock into the opening. They built a trestle above the opening. They dumped tons of rock down, building from both sides toward the center. At first all went well. On both sides the dams held and the channel of the Chagres narrowed. But then they struck a snag. The Chagres was moving more and more swiftly through the narrow opening. It

80

picked up the rocks and swept them downriver. What was worse, the rainy season was about to begin.

The engineers had to do something in a hurry. What they decided to do was risky. They dumped carloads of twisted iron rails into the opening to keep the rocks from rolling. They knew one of two things would happen; the dam would hold, or the Chagres would tear out everything—dam, trestle and all. They dumped the tangled masses of twisted rails. They watched the Chagres hiss and foam through them. The engineers must have kept their fingers crossed as they dumped tons of rock on the upstream side. The dam held. The Chagres returned to its original riverbed.

The dam at Gatun had to do two things. It had to hold back the Chagres; it had to withstand possible earthquakes. There are no live volcanoes in Panama, but there are occasional earth-quakes. The dam at Gatun covers 288 acres. It is an earth-fill dam—an artificial hill, a mile-and-a-half long, a half a mile wide at the base, 105 feet high. It contains 21 million cubic feet of earth and rock. A two-horse wagon can handle one cubic yard of earth. That gives one some idea of the size of the dam!

Each time a ship crosses Panama 52 million gallons of water pour into the locks to raise the ship to Gatun Lake and lower it again to the sea. It takes big pipes to carry that water to the locks fast enough. First, culverts run lengthwise through the walls of the locks. They are eighteen feet in diameter, big enough for an express train to run through. Fourteen cross culverts run under the floor of each lock. They are big enough for a two-horse wagon to go through. Then 70 openings, each as big around as a sugar barrel, carry the water into each lock.

The Americans had come to Panama in 1904. The digging of the canal did not get under way, full tilt, until 1907. But by New Year's Day of 1913 the engineers were on fire with a dream. What if they could open the canal the fall of 1913, on the 400th anniversary of the day Balboa

Center culverts in each wall of Gatun Locks are eighteen feet in diameter.

reached the Pacific! They could see the end of all the jobs now: dams, locks, gates, channels dredged to deep water at each end of the canal . . . They could do it! They had tamed the Chagres! They had conquered mountains! They had . . . Then in January of 1913 a vast slide poured into Culebra Cut.

Once more the steam shovels set to work. Months passed. By September of 1913 they had barely made a dent in the mass.

There was a ceremony on that 400th anniversary: President Wilson pressed a button in the White House. A signal traveled by telegraph line and cable to Culebra. It set off tons of dynamite. The charge blew out the temporary dam between Gatun Lake and Culebra Cut. Now

Landslide in Culebra Cut held up the completion of the Canal for many months.

the waters of the Chagres would flow both into the Atlantic and into the Pacific.

But ships could not cross Panama. There was work for the Chagres to do. Colonel Goethals had decided he could move the spoil faster by using dredges instead of steam shovels.

A fleet of dredges, moored side by side, began to scoop out the spoil. Double crews worked night and day. It was May of 1914—sixteen months after the slide—before even a barge could go through Culebra Cut.

On August 15, 1914, a ship made the first official ocean-to-ocean crossing. She was the *Ancon*, a freighter that had hauled supplies to the Canal Zone all during the building.

How long the world had waited for that historic day! But the crossing of the *Ancon* passed almost without notice. Other news filled the papers: World War I had begun. That was why the formal "opening" of the canal did not come until 1920, after hundreds of ships had been passing through it for several years.

Panama Canal Information Office

10. Today

Let us take an imaginary trip through the canal from the Atlantic to the Pacific. Our ship waits in Limón Bay for a pilot to come aboard. He takes charge. We follow a channel through the bay and inland to Gatun. In front of us are the huge locks.

Now our motors or engines are stopped. Powerful electric locomotives, called "mules," wait on tracks on each side of the locks. Four or more of the mules, depending on the size of our ship, will pull us through the locks. The mules

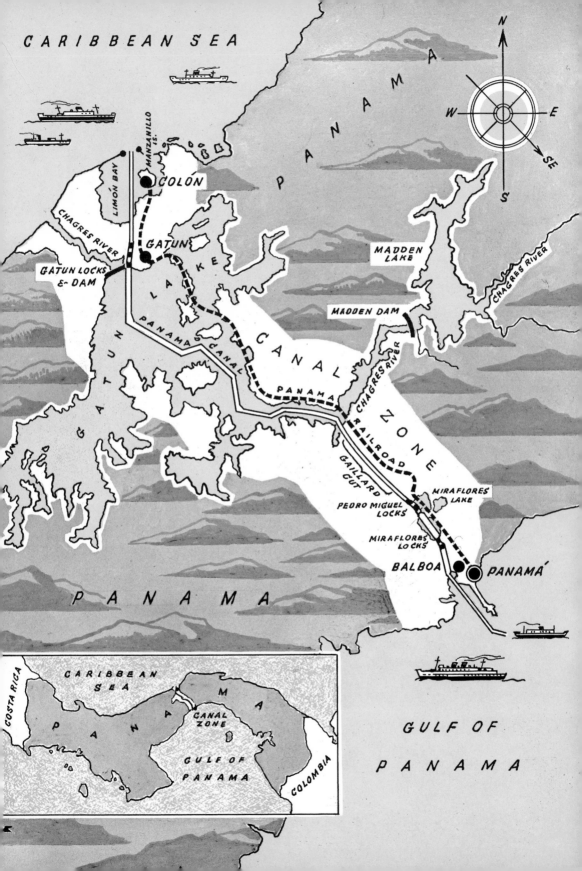

Panama Canal Information Office

Gatun Locks form twin flights of three steps each which raise and lower ships 85 feet.

are attached to the ship with strong cables, two forward to tow her, two aft to keep her in the center of her path, and more between if they are needed.

The gates of the first lock open. The water is level with the water in the channel. The mules tow us in. Behind us the great gates close. The water boils up, filling the lock, raising our ship. When our ship is high enough to float into the next lock the water stops flowing. The forward gates open. The mules tow us into the second lock, and then into the third. The waters in the third lock rise until we are on a level with the surface of Gatun Lake—85 feet above sea level.

The mules turn us loose. We sail under our own power across Lake Gatun. We are busy watching the lovely wooded islands and hillocks that dot the lake. The pilot is busy watching the pairs of lighthouses that guide him along his zig-zag course across the lake. The towers are in pairs, one rising high behind the other. When the pilot has them lined up one behind the other, he knows he is in his channel. Presently two more towers appear off to one side. He knows he is coming to a bend in the channel. He changes course until the second pair of towers is lined up, one behind the other. He starts watching for the next pair. He will change course eight times crossing the lake.

The crossing of the lake is probably the most beautiful part of the trip; going through Culebra Cut—now Gaillard Cut—is certainly the most awe-inspiring. Here a man-made chasm nine

Aerial view of Gaillard Cut shows it to be an enormous man-made ditch.

miles long goes through mountains that sometimes rise more than 500 feet above us.

At the end of Gaillard Cut our ship again stops. We are at Pedro Miguel, ready to enter another lock. Again the mules take us in tow. This time the water does not rise; it goes down. We have come upstairs to Lake Gatun; we are going downstairs now to sea level. We leave the

Panama Canal Information Office

Pedro Miguel Locks as seen from Gaillard Cut, looking toward Miraflores Lake.

lock, cross a little lake—Miraflores—then mules take us in tow again and take us through the last two locks at Miraflores. We are at sea level again in the channel that leads to deep water in the Pacific. A leisurely smooth-water trip of 50 miles has saved us thousands of miles around Cape Horn.

In round numbers the Chagres River saves

8,000 miles between New York and San Francisco, 7,000 between New York and Honolulu, 6,000 miles between New York and Callao (the seaport of Lima, Peru), and 4,000 miles between New York and Valparaiso (the main port of Chile).

If our ship were making the voyage from New Orleans, the Chagres would save 9,000 miles to San Francisco, 8,000 miles to Honolulu, 7,000

Inside view of a lock control house, showing lock control levers in the foreground and a timetable for transits on the wall. Traffic control plans are prepared daily.

Courtesy of United Fruit Company

miles to Callao, and 5,000 miles to Valparaiso.

The Chagres has furnished 52 million gallons of water to carry our one ship through the locks. Moreover it has furnished the electric power to run 100 or more motors. It has opened and closed the gigantic gates of the locks. Those gates are 7 feet thick, 65 feet wide, and from 47 to 82 feet high. They weigh from 390 to 730 tons each. The Chagres has furnished the power to open and shut all the valves that control the flow of the water. It has furnished the power for all the mules that tow ships through the locks. It furnishes electricity to light all the houses and shops of the Canal Zone, and the lighthouses, beacons and buoys of the canal.

But suppose you were an Inquiring Reporter. You asked the Man on Deck near you, "Where is the Chagres River?" He might say, "I don't know."

Suppose you asked him, "Who was John F. Stevens?" He might say again, "I don't know. Who was he?" If you had time to visit Balboa

A new addition in the Canal Zone is the Thatcher Ferry Bridge which crosses the Canal at Balboa on the Pacific end.

you could show him a statue of Mr. Stevens. On its base is a quotation from Colonel Goethals: "The canal is his monument."

Men finally got around to recognizing the brains behind the job. I wonder . . . will they ever erect a statue to the Chagres—the power behind the Panama Canal?

Index

Meet the Author

JEAN LEE LATHAM, author of over 30 published children's books, was born in Buckhannon, West Virginia, and now lives in Coral Gables, Florida. She says, "I write because that's what I like to do more than anything else." To her writing, however, she brings a rich and varied background.

Among other things, Miss Latham has been a linotype operator and the editor of a play-publishing company. During World War II she was in charge of training Signal Corps inspectors and received the War Department Silver Wreath for her work. She also was a Red Cross Gray Lady for a number of years.

An author of plays as well as books, Miss Latham has written for the stage, radio and television. She has received several honors for her books, including the coveted Newbery Award. Jean Lee Latham is the author of *Eli Whitney: Great Inventor* and *Samuel F. B. Morse: Artist-Inventor*, both in Garrard's Discovery Book series.